Kobe during the national anthem at the Staples Center. He told "Dear Basketball" animator Glen Keane he once based his strategy in a championship game on the rhythms of Beethoven's Fifth Symphony.

Kobe fist-bumps his daughter Gianna after his final NBA game. He scored 60 points as the Lakers won 101-96.

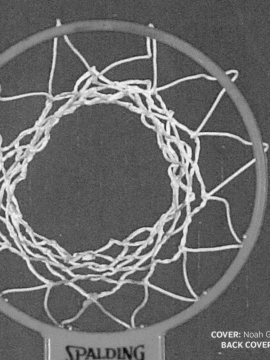

IN MEMORIAM

KOBE
BRYANT

AUGUST 23, 1978 — JANUARY 26, 2020

A celebration of the life, legacy and immense talent of
the Black Mamba: one of the greatest to ever grace the court.

THE MAMBA'S LIFE

In just 41 years, Kobe Bryant managed to accomplish more than most could if they lived to be 100.

1978

AUGUST 23, 1978
Kobe Bryant is born to Joe "Jellybean" Bryant and Pam Bryant. Joe is a professional basketball player whose career takes the family to Italy in 1984. Much of Kobe's childhood will be spent in the European country.

WINTER-SPRING 1996
Kobe, playing all five positions, leads the Lower Merion High School Aces to their first Pennsylvania state championship in 53 years.

NOVEMBER 3, 1996
Kobe makes his NBA debut, playing six minutes for the Lakers against the Minnesota Timberwolves. His first professional points will come days later against the New York Knicks.

OCTOBER 31, 1997
The Lakers begin their 1997-98 campaign against the Utah Jazz. In Kobe's second season, he begins to take a more active role in the Lakers' offense, more than doubling his average ppg.

APRIL 18, 2001
Kobe Bryant marries Vanessa Laine at St. Edward the Confessor R.C. Church in Dana Point, California. They will go on to have four daughters.

JUNE 15, 2004
In what many view as one of the more shocking sports events in the 2000s, the Lakers lose in the NBA Finals to the Detroit Pistons.

91 — 92 — 93 — 94 — 95 — 96 — 97 — 98 — 99 — 00 — 01 — 02 — 03 — 04 — 05 — 06

1991
The Bryants return to the U.S. from Italy, settling in Philadelphia, PA. The following year, Kobe enrolls at Lower Merion High School, where he will attract the attention of both college and professional scouts with his skill and passion.

JUNE 26, 1996
Shortly after his graduation from Lower Merion High School, Kobe announces that he plans to "take my talents to the NBA." He is selected 13th overall in the 1996 NBA Draft by the Charlotte Hornets. He is then traded to the Los Angeles Lakers, the franchise for which he will suit up throughout his career.

FEBRUARY 8, 1997
Kobe, in his rookie year, wins the 1997 Slam Dunk Contest.

NOVEMBER 2, 1999
With new coach Phil Jackson at the helm, Bryant and the Lakers begin their 1999-2000 season. The Bulls' mastermind of the 1990s, coupled with the earlier acquisition of all-star center Shaquille O'Neal, help Los Angeles reignite their "Showtime" image and win the first of three championships in a row.

JUNE 12, 2002
Kobe and the Lakers win their third Championship in a row when they defeat the Eastern Conference Champion New Jersey Nets.

OCTOBER 31, 2006
Kobe makes his debut as #24, having traded his old jersey number for one he wore in youth basketball.

MARCH 4, 2018
Kobe's short film, "Dear Basketball," based on a poem he'd written to announce his retirement in 2015, wins an Academy Award.

OCTOBER 23, 2018
Bryant's book *The Mamba Mentality: How I Play* hits shelves.

AUGUST 24, 2008
As a member of the U.S. Men's Basketball Olympic Team in Beijing, Kobe wins his first Gold Medal.

FEBRUARY 1, 2011
Kobe becomes one of only seven players in NBA history to record 25,000 points, 5,000 rebounds and 5,000 assists.

APRIL 12, 2013
A ruptured Achilles Tendon ends Kobe's season, but he stays on the court to take his foul shots on one leg after the injury. He sinks them both.

07 — 08 — 09 — 10 — 11 — 12 — 13 — 14 — 15 — 16 — 17 — 18 — 19 — 20

JUNE 14, 2009
Kobe leads the Lakers to their first title of the post-Shaq era in a Finals MVP-winning performance.

AUGUST 12, 2012
As a member of the U.S. Men's Basketball team in London, Bryant wins his second Olympic gold.

NOVEMBER 2, 2012
With his 1,725th steal, Kobe overtakes Magic Johnson as the Lakers' all-time leader.

NOVEMBER 30, 2014
When he records a triple-double against the Toronto Raptors, Bryant becomes the oldest player in NBA history to score 30 points with 10 rebounds and 10 assists.

JANUARY 26, 2020
Kobe Bryant is killed in a helicopter crash in Calabasas, California, on his way to a basketball camp. His 13-year-old daughter, Gianna, also loses her life in the crash.

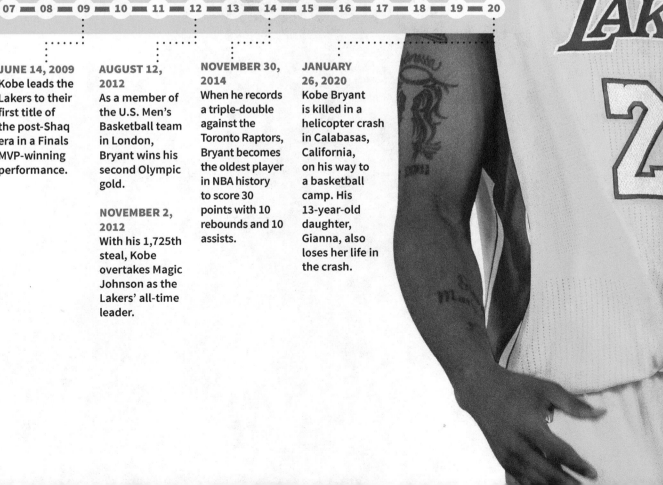

Kobe during the pre-game ceremony on January 11, 2006, as the Lakers took on the Portland Trail Blazers. He would go on to score 41 that night.

THE ENIGMA REMAINS

Kobe Bryant was taken from the basketball
world on the cusp of his elder statesmanship.
The game, and those who love it, will never forget.

When the basketball faithful are faced with world-shaking news of any kind, we tend to look to a few distinguished elders for their guidance. It's one of the great things about athletics: because retirements tend to be so long, several generations of these elders are in the public eye at a given time, offering varied perspectives and growing in wisdom even as they decline somewhat in athletic prowess. No matter what the news is, be it a trade, a protest, a scandalous draft pick or a draft pick steeped in scandal, fans of the sport can find a well-executed argument to sway them from one of these elders. That's why looking to the usual sources—Kareem Abdul-Jabbar, Bill Russell, Magic Johnson, Walt Frazier et al.—for words that could help make sense of the passing of Kobe Bryant at age 41 on January 26, 2020, was both disappointing and understandable. For all their skill, experience and personal anecdotes about how the game ought to be played, they were as shocked and speechless as the rest of us, trying just as hard as fans to wrap their minds around an unimaginable tragedy. Not only had Kobe's chance to join their ranks been violently taken away, but eight other people were lost along with him—among them Kobe's 13-year-old daughter Gianna.

Kobe was for 20 years not only one of the most dominant players the NBA had ever seen but also one of the quietest. In a game where off-court style can be just as much of a headline grabber as on-court performance, Kobe famously kept to himself. His February 2015 interview with Chuck Klosterman for *GQ*, in which he delved deep into his personal life, was both an aberration and a revelation. The still waters of the Black Mamba's mind were even deeper than we had imagined, and the frank discussion of basketball and philosophy heralded his arrival as one of the newest of basketball's revered elders.

What President Obama referred to as Kobe's promising "Second Act" in his first memorial message was poised to rival any of the greatest in the game. He showed us that at the Oscars when, a new kind of trophy in hand, he promised he'd never "Shut up and dribble." His passion, built through 20 years of fairytale success and intense drama in Hollywood, was to tell stories. According to Klosterman, his idea of the ideal modern story, one that would touch as many people as possible, was unique: "Bryant views branding as a modern form of 'storytelling.' I note that this comparison is only partially accurate, since branding is a form of storytelling with a conscious commercial purpose. 'For some,' he concedes. 'But that's not a universal thing. That's like saying every wizard within Slytherin House is a villain.'"

For someone who spent a fair amount of time in his career contending with harsh critics painting him as just such a figure, Kobe was at least as self-aware as he was deemed aloof. He knew people thought he shot too much, noting

he'd been hearing that since he was an 8-year-old. But didn't people complain Mozart included too many notes in his compositions? Yes, he might have been difficult to get along with in more intense moments of perfectionism. But he was just as quick to recognize this as a weakness, as he did to Klosterman, as some might have been with

a justification. After all, it was difficult to argue with the on-court results.

That *GQ* interview begins with the following: "'I know who I am,' is among the first things Kobe Bryant tells me, which is the kind of statement made only by people who are very, very right or very, very wrong." Kobe was the former. But

deep in strategic conversation with his daughter Gianna—nicknamed "Mambacita"—it's tragically clear that his priority in life was passing that knowledge to his daughters rather than the world at large. For most of us, the iceberg that was Kobe's mind will remain 7/8 underwater. What we have is, most importantly, what he meant to us—and by extension what the game of basketball means to us.

As Kareem Abdul-Jabbar insinuated in his initial memorial message, Kobe changed the fundamental makeup of the game. He took games into his own hands in a way that even the greatest big men could seldom do, let alone guards. He eschewed the exploitation of the NCAA in favor of steady work when few recruits were willing to stand up to the college-to-pro system. In an era when skeptics wondered if there would ever be a player as explosive as Michael Jordan, Kobe showed up and proved that MJ had inspired a generation that could produce its own superstar. Kids in the early 2000s weren't yelling "Jordan!" when they tossed scrap paper or apple cores into the trash from a distance: They were yelling "Kobe." They still are.

He's the Black Mamba. Mr. 81. Kobe-wan Kenobi. He's the kid who took Brandy to the prom, followed KG's lead and went straight to the pros, then won the Slam Dunk contest as if to prove he belonged. The cut-your-heart-out sharpshooter who never saw a pass he wouldn't have preferred to turn into a jump shot; and the guy who wouldn't have considered that statement a criticism. The unflinching defender whose game face suffered no fools (just ask Matt Barnes). The Laker team leader who hung his 2008 gold medal in teammate (and silver medalist Team Spain leader) Pau Gasol's locker at the start of the season to both mock and motivate him. The point guard who talked about basketball not in points, but in symphonic movements—Beethoven's Fifth apparently inspired him to utterly destroy the other team. He is all these things. It's hard to write he *was*.

It's almost as difficult to describe the inevitability basketball fans felt about the Lakers in the aughts. Kobe leaving the ground

he had only just begun to share exactly what he knew with the world when his time was cut short. His book *Mamba Mentality: How I Play* gives us a glimpse, but it's also more of a debut to the world of analysis than a final word on the subject of how Kobe approached life. Watching footage of him on the sidelines of an AAU game,

Dallas Mavericks' Josh Howard, right, gets called for a foul against Kobe in his virtuosic solo performance against the Mavericks in 2005.

for a jumper was the basketball equivalent of Thanos snapping his fingers in the Marvel Universe: devastation for everyone not on his side. And on the rare occasions when the first attempt failed, Shaq or Gasol were there to clean up with the rebound. The Lakers, after floundering for their first few post-Magic years, were once again a touchstone for basketball fans across the globe. In the most watched city on the planet, the most talented basketball player was taking the biggest share of the spotlight. This magazine is full of moments in which Kobe shocked the basketball universe with sheer skill, from his 81-point massacre of the Raptors to his four consecutive 50-point games to his team-leading Finals assists. But for us, there is no moment that better defines the Black Mamba than December 20, 2005.

Just a few weeks before the aforementioned 81-point rampage, Kobe proved that when he was in the zone, no team on Earth could stop him, let alone individual opponent. When Kobe checked out of the game for the last time that night after only three quarters, he had 62 points. The Dallas Mavericks had 61. Like the snake (or Tarantino-penned assassin) from which he drew his nickname, Kobe struck fast and by instinct, releasing all the venom he could, all at once. He was once a prodigiously talented kid who challenged grown men to one-on-ones. As a pro it often seemed like he was challenging the entire opposition at the same time. Of his generation, only Kobe's friend Tiger Woods came close to him in terms of sheer will to win. Moments of brilliance like these will be with fans forever, confined to the basketball court though they may be. But the heartbreak of losing such a great mind just as it was turned outside itself will last just as long, especially in LA, where fans feel they've lost a captain and a surrogate coach at the same time. It's a rare professional athlete who, upon retiring, can say that his future is just as bright as his past. Kobe could. That's why the suddenness of his death has affected the world so acutely: his legacy was complete, yet somehow just beginning to take shape.

"MAKE HIS MEMORY LAST FOREVER"

As they mourned Kobe, fans called for the NBA to honor him with a unique tribute.

Tens of thousands of people have signed a petition to get the NBA to replace its existing logo with one incorporating Kobe Bryant.

Throughout his 20-year career in the NBA, Kobe became one of the sport's most successful and recognizable players. He picked up Michael Jordan's mantle as the best player in the league and, like Jordan's, his profile transcended the sport and spread far beyond the NBA's borders.

In two decades with the Los Angeles Lakers Kobe won five NBA titles, was twice named MVP of the NBA Finals and won the regular season MVP in 2008. An 18-time All-Star selection, Kobe won two Olympic golds and ranks fourth in the all-time scoring list. Launched on *change.org*, the petition aims to get the Black Mamba forever enshrined on the NBA logo.

"With the untimely and unexpected passing of Kobe Bryant please sign this petition in an attempt to make his memory last forever as the NBA logo," petition organizer Nick M. explained.

The petition has set itself a target of 3 million signatures and has been signed more than 2 million times at the time of press.

Save for a small change to the typeface, which was introduced in 2017, the NBA has used its iconic tri-color logo since 1971. Created by Alan Siegel—the same man who had overseen the design of the Major League Baseball's logo—the NBA logo incorporates the silhouette of Los Angeles Lakers great Jerry West. The logo is based on a picture of West taken by Wen Roberts and shows the former guard dribbling.

"It had a nice flavor to it," Siegel told the *Los Angeles Times* in 2010. "So I took that picture, and we traced it. It was perfect. It was vertical and it had a sense of movement. It was just one of those things that clicked."

The NBA, however, has always officially denied the logo is based on a particular player. West has previously suggested that it was time for another player to appear on the logo.

Perhaps that time has come.

From the *Newsweek* Archive 1/27/20
By Dan Cancian

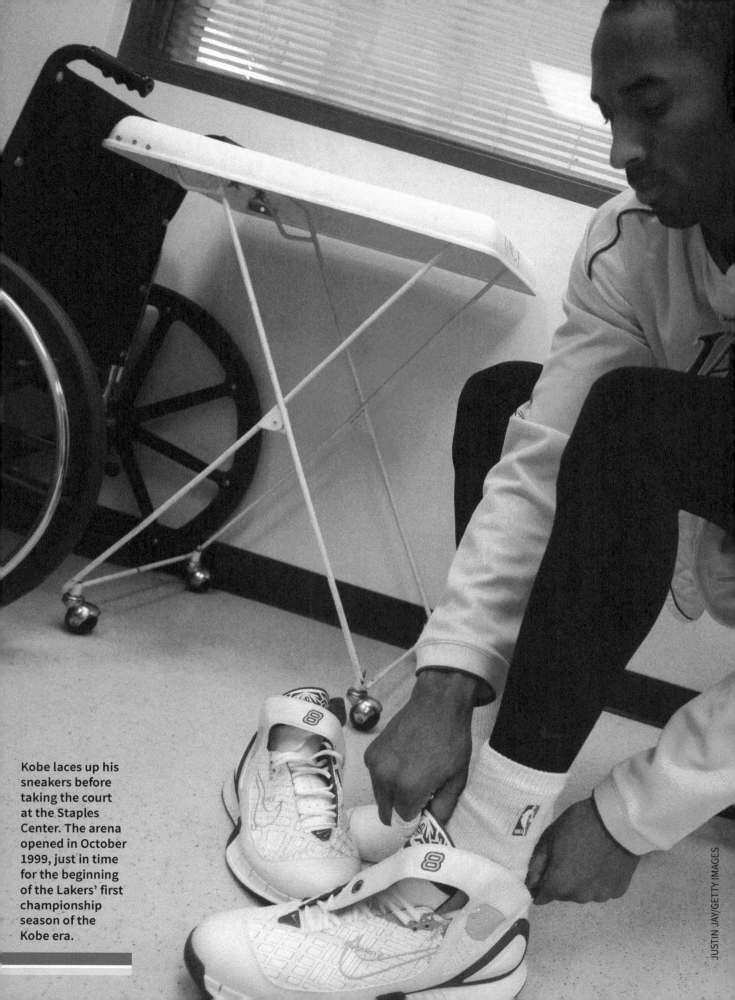

Kobe laces up his sneakers before taking the court at the Staples Center. The arena opened in October 1999, just in time for the beginning of the Lakers' first championship season of the Kobe era.

A young Kobe shows off during practice in Lower Merion's gym on January 19, 1996. As a pro, Kobe was an ambassador for After School All-Stars, a non-profit providing after-school programs to children in 13 U.S. cities.

TEENAGE ALL-STAR

Kobe Bryant was an early-bloomer—a fact his high school opponents learned very quickly.

After a childhood spent abroad watching his father's professional career, Kobe Bryant had developed an intense love for the game as well as the kind of skills only an insider willing to put in untold effort can acquire. So when he matriculated at Lower Merion High School in Philadelphia, Kobe was ready to start impressing his public. An extremely rare freshman selected for the Lower Merion varsity team, Kobe was a standout in his first season, but the team suffered a losing season. It would be their only such campaign during Kobe's tenure at Lower Merion.

Over the next three seasons, Kobe would play all five positions as he led the Lower Merion Aces to a combined record of 77-13. During these years he was named Pennsylvania's Player of the Year and began attracting the interest of both college and pro scouts. When he saw Kevin

Garnett go straight from high school to the first round of the NBA draft, Kobe's mind was made up. But he had one more hill to climb as a high school player: Lower Merion hadn't won a state championship in more than 50 years.

During a senior season that began with an MVP award at the Adidas ABCD Camp, Kobe averaged 30 points and 12 rebounds a game. The Aces' first championship in 53 years was the icing on Kobe's graduation cake. He was also the recipient of the Naismith High School Player of the Year award, Gatorade Men's National Basketball Player of the Year award, a McDonald's All-American nomination, a first-team Parade All-American spot and a *USA Today* All-USA First Team election. With 2,883 high school career points, he was the most prolific scorer in Southeastern Pennsylvania history. And the NBA was calling.

Kobe Bryant announces he is foregoing college and will enter the NBA draft at a press conference in the Lower Merion High School Gym. In 1996, *USA Today* named Kobe the National High School Player of the Year.

STRAIGHT OUTTA HIGH SCHOOL

When Kobe did it, coming to the NBA from 12th grade was still looked on as a gamble: But he proved he was more than ready for the pros.

After declaring for the 1996 NBA Draft, Kobe Bryant became one of the most talked-about prospects since Michael Jordan. Could this 17-year-old phenom really play with the top few hundred basketball players in the world? At pre-draft workouts in Los Angeles, Kobe impressed upon Laker executive Jerry West that he could. According to a 2000 interview with the *Long Beach Press-Telegram*, West said Kobe "marched" all over NBA veterans during these sessions and wowed the Laker legend enough to consider making the young man a part of his LA powerhouse.

So on the day before the draft, the Lakers contacted the Charlotte Hornets about securing the rights to their 13th pick in exchange for veteran center Vlade Divac. As the clock wound down on draft night, the Lakers instructed the Hornets to pick a high school point guard whom the Charlotte club hadn't even been seriously scouting. Kobe Bryant would spend the next 20 seasons in Los Angeles, winning five titles and accumulating more points than all but three players in NBA history.

He scored no points in his first official action, coming in off the bench for roughly six minutes during a game against the Minnesota Timberwolves; he logged a block and one steal. He would eventually start six games, and at the end of his first season averaged 7 points and 15 minutes per game. He was named to the NBA All-Rookie Second Team, and when he took home the title in that season's Slam Dunk contest during the NBA's All-Star weekend, sports columnists across the country were doing their damnedest to name him the "'Air' Apparent" to Michael Jordan before anyone else could steal the pun.

All in all, his season showed incredible promise, though it also included flashes of the growth he'd require in order to become one of the league's most feared players. During Game 5 of the Lakers' conference semifinal series against the Utah Jazz, Kobe showed flashes of brilliance, but also shot a few gut-churning air balls during overtime, sealing the series for the Jazz. The Lakers were out of the quest for the championship. But their star rookie, the youngest starter in NBA history, had enough brash confidence to declare they'd be back.

THE 1996 NBA DRAFT

Kobe and those who went before him in 1996 represent an era: journeyman and legend alike.

1. Allen Iverson
2. Marcus Camby
3. Shareef Abdur-Rahim
4. Stephon Marbury
5. Ray Allen
6. Antoine Walker
7. Lorenzen Wright
8. Kerry Kittles
9. Samaki Walker
10. Erick Dampier
11. Todd Fuller
12. Vitaly Potapenko
13. Kobe Bryant

RUSTY KENNEDY/AP IMAGES

KOBE'S ARRIVAL

Competing against the likes of Ray Allen, Chris Carr, Darvin Ham, Michael Finley and Bob Sura, Kobe Bryant announced his debut as a star at Cleveland's Gund Arena for the 1997 Slam Dunk Contest. After the first round of the contest, which judges players based on the difficulty and style of their dunks, Kobe trailed Carr by seven points. But Kobe had saved his best for the final round, and pulled ahead by four points with an insane self-pass reverse tomahawk from the corner. The 1997 Slam Dunk crown would be Kobe's first bit of NBA hardware, but there was a lot more in his future.

Kobe plays against the Phoenix Suns at the Great Western Forum in Inglewood, California, on March 24, 1999. The Lakers would soon move to the Staples Center, where they remain.

KOBE GOES IT ALONE

Before he was the owner of several championship rings and the NBA's top accolades, *Newsweek* profiled a (transformatively talented) kid trying to find his footing in the league.

A t the end of the Los Angeles Lakers' tumultuous season, Kobe Bryant will, as he has after every game and practice, "get ghost." Nobody exits the LA Forum swifter than Kobe, signing a few autographs on the fly 'til he disappears behind the tinted windows of his jet-black Mercedes coupe. Sanctuary lies a few miles up the coast in a sprawling, six-bedroom Pacific Palisades manse, where Kobe lives with his parents and an older sister. In his bedroom, with the Italian marble floor, the Jacuzzi and the spectacular ocean view, Kobe retreats into reverie in which there are only triumphs. "Like that game against Houston [in the 1999 playoffs] where I made those free throws at the end of the game and we won," says Kobe. "I've dreamed about that many times. I like to dream about it again."

At 20, Bryant is already living the modern American dream, a $70 million man on the NBA's glamour team in the nation's starriest city. His acrobatic moves make him the envy of teenage boys and his good looks and megawatt smile a heartthrob for teenage girls, ensuring his status as one of the NBA's premier pitchmen (Adidas, Sprite). While this season, his third, was arguably his finest, he has found himself out of sync—on and off the floor—with his team. He has been publicly criticized for his poor judgment on the court. And he is stuck in an ugly rivalry with the team's other superstar, Shaquille O'Neal. Despite his considerable

boyish charm, Kobe says he doesn't have a single close friend on the team or even in the city. All those hours in his room, where Kobe daydreams, plays videogames and writes some rap, can't assuage this painful dissonance. "It's been a really difficult year for my son," says Joe Bryant, himself a former NBA journeyman. "We can't do anything about it but give him hugs and kisses and lots of support when he gets home."

When Kobe opted to skip college for the NBA, many questioned whether the Philadelphia-area high-schooler was ready. But their reservations were largely about his game. It proved to be stellar, as his numbers (19.9 points, 5.3 rebounds and 3.8 assists per game in '99) and all-star status attest. Last year L.A. fans chanted him into the starting lineup ("Ko-be, Ko-be"), overriding the then Lakers coach Del Harris's plans to ease him into the limelight. And he now stands, or soars, as the most credible Air apparent to Michael Jordan.

But Kobe clearly wasn't prepared for the NBA's bruising emotional battles. "No doubt college would have helped both emotionally and physically for Kobe," says Lakers executive Jerry West. Bryant is, at times, wistful about that missed opportunity. He talked regularly with University of Connecticut star Richard Hamilton this season, enjoying vicariously Hamilton's NCAA championship run with the Huskies. "I watched it and thought about how I would have done that play, and then I'd tell Richard about

"WE DON'T NEED A RELATIONSHIP OFF THE COURT," SAYS O'NEAL. "WE DON'T HAVE TO BE BUDDIES."

it," says Kobe, who met Hamilton at a high-school tournament. "We do a lot of trash talking. I tell him if I'd been there I would have kicked his butt and he would have never made it to the Final Four."

Instead, Kobe endured the Lakers' roller-coaster season and a harsh backlash, from teammates and media, that has stunned him. "If you really look at my numbers, they're pretty good. And no one is thinking about how I really

just got into the game, that I'm still learning and I'm going to make mistakes," says Kobe. "People don't know my game and what I need to do for myself to get better. Sometimes what they say may be true, but you get to a point where you hear and you don't hear."

Despite the patient tutelage of his coaches and the sometimes loud and obscene reminders from other Lakers, Bryant has often been in the don't-hear mode, going solo on the court,

Kobe and Shaq late in the 4th quarter during Game 1 of the 2001 NBA Western Conference first round play-off against the Portland Trail Blazers. Their win that year in the Finals was their second of three in a row after this article first appeared in *Newsweek*.

seemingly unaware of his teammates. And Kobe, who grew up in Italy while his father played pro ball there, can "not hear" in three languages. After one game, in which Kobe failed to pass to a teammate who was wide open under the basket, the player screamed at Kobe in the locker room, "If you ever do that again, I'll kick your motherf---ing --s."

Bryant admits he takes too many wild shots and too often plays to the crowd. ("I would hear them and just run wild.") Still, he's got a stubborn streak and remains supremely confident in his own abilities. He doesn't understand why his teammates get upset about his shot selection. "If the shot loses the game, it's affecting me too," he says. "I'm a part of the team."

Nobody has been affected more by Kobe's star turn than O'Neal, the team captain. Shaq, who like many of the game's great big men has that "nobody likes Godzilla" chip on his shoulder, wasn't prepared for the passion with which Laker fans embraced the new kid. "His instant stardom, the way the crowd took to Kobe, really hurt him," says one Laker. "Shaquille was supposed to be the marquee player." The two had a physical altercation on court this preseason in which O'Neal slapped Kobe in the face—"no big deal," they both say now—and they don't talk to each other if they can help it. "We don't need a relationship off the court," says O'Neal. "We don't have to be buddies."

Kobe agrees and extends that concept to his relationship with all his teammates. "We may not be close off the court, but I've got their back on the court no matter what," he says. Before the playoffs began, the Lakers held a team meeting to try to ease tensions and get the other players to give Kobe more support. "We look at all the attention and hype he gets and think he shouldn't be making all those mistakes," said Laker forward Rick Fox. "But we forget he's just a kid. We just sort of left him hanging this season, an island by himself, and that's going to stop. He wants to win as much as anyone else, and he deserves our support."

L.A. routed Houston in the first round of the playoffs, and the Lakers staff judged the team therapy a rousing success. "This has been the first time when Kobe definitely understood the team concept and embraced it," says Lakers assistant coach Larry Drew. But there were still some bumps in the court. Asked about the shackling of Rockets forward Scottie Pippen, who was defended brilliantly by Kobe, Shaq grumbled, "Whoever was guarding Pippen was doing a good job." The biggest bump came in the next round against San Antonio when, despite scoring 28 points, Kobe bricked two crucial free throws, enabling the Spurs to win in the final seconds. After the misses, Kobe flashed a schoolboy's sheepish grin. Later he waxed philosophical: "We've been through so much this year, I think it would be kind of an odd feeling if it wasn't an uphill battle."

Former Laker great Magic Johnson has counseled both Shaq and Kobe, telling them that it will always be an uphill battle unless the two can coalesce, as he and Kareem Abdul-Jabbar did to lead the Laker championship teams of the '80s. But O'Neal is skeptical about comparison. "They made me captain, so that's that," he said. "Any time Kobe wants to become Magic Johnson, I'll step aside, but until then we have to use the people we have the best way we can." Magic also believes that the current Laker team will never truly click on the floor until Kobe hangs with his teammates off the floor. L.A. is a party team, hitting the hot spots like the Shark Bar or the Century Club and a ceaseless parade of private affairs. But Kobe isn't interested. "I'm not out there trying to be Hollywood and club-hopping," says Kobe, who can't drink legally. "Even when I turn 21, I don't see it changing."

Kobe says he's a loner by nature. At the Forum he dresses separately in a back room; on the road, he sticks to his hotel room, filling his day with repeat breakfasts—eggs, potatoes and pancakes morning, noon and night—and pay-per-view movies. Kobe is also something of a misfit among the young black men who populate the NBA, the result, he says, of having been raised first in Italy and then in an affluent white suburb. His tastes span hip-hop, Alanis Morissette and *Star Wars* movies. Though he was a superstar jock who led his school to its first state basketball crown in 53 years, Kobe remembers high school as an often awkward and painful time. "When I first got back to the States, I barely spoke English, so that made me odd man out from the jump," he says. "Combine that with Black people having their own way of talking, and I really had to learn two languages in order to fit. Kids are cruel. It's always been hard."

It was hard, too, in Italy, where the Bryants were one of the few American families—and the only black one—in their town. "We really began to rely heavily on each other because we were all we had," says Sharia, 23, his oldest sister.

Such family-centric notions are very Italian, and Kobe has come to idealize the Italian experience and recall it as the happiest time of his life. He vacations there each summer. And he talks about marrying young (even though he has no current girlfriend), having lots of bambinos and raising them in Italy. "My kids could grow up without all this fear of shooting in the school and that type of madness," he says. "I would like that type of happiness or peace."

He doesn't have it now. Indeed, asked if he's happy, Kobe shrugs and says, "I guess, maybe. Not really." Then he adds rather poignantly, "I really don't believe in happiness." Still, family remains a sustaining force, and Kobe sounds like very much the big kid he is when he says nothing beats going home and "bugging my sisters." He couldn't comprehend why Sharia, who is married with a 4-month-old daughter, chose to move out of their house. He dotes on his niece, Tayah. "He's not your typical guy or basketball player—out chasing girls," says Sharia. "I'm proud of that." On a road trip to Orlando, while the rest of the team was club-hopping, Bryant was buying out the Disney World store for Tayah.

But there are ways in which Bryant is typical of his NBA generation, another cocksure kid intent on dazzling us with his game. Joe Bryant insists that the decision to turn pro—"to take my talent to the NBA" was how Kobe put it—was strictly his son's. "He really wanted to, and you have to let your children do what they want," says his father. Kobe was drafted by the Charlotte Hornets and, much as Shaq did in Orlando, would have benefited from playing in a less pressured environment. However, his management team, which included his dad, forced a trade to L.A., where Kobe could also pursue options in the entertainment industry. (He has a recording contract for a rap album, but hasn't finished it yet.) Ex-Laker coach Harris was frustrated during Kobe's rookie season by what he viewed as a mismatch. "Here's this kid in a man's game and he's not ready," fretted Harris. "He should be on another team that isn't expected to win right now."

Kobe waits for the ball in a February 14, 1999, game against the Indiana Pacers. The following year, the Lakers would beat the Pacers in the Finals.

"THERE ARE TIMES WHEN I GO HOME AND THINK THE LORD HAS GIVEN ME A LOT TO DEAL WITH"

Kobe acknowledges it might have been easier to have entered the NBA elsewhere. But he believes the trial-by-fire in L.A. has both hastened his basketball development and forced him to grow up faster. Kobe is the first to say that, however much consternation there is in his life, his coming of age should never be confused with real tragedy. "There are times when I go home and think the Lord has given me a lot to deal with," he says. "But I always come to the conclusion that he would never put more of a burden on a person's shoulders than they are ready to bear." And those times he isn't quite ready, well, he can always go to his room.

From the *Newsweek* Archive 5/30/99
By Allison Samuels

THE 2000 NBA CHAMPIONSHIP

YOUNG KOBE GETS HIS RING

Kobe and Shaq had led the Lakers to one of their best starts in franchise history for the 1999-2000 season: a 33-7 record for their first 40 games. And with both of their stars healthy, the Lake Show was able to continue well into the postseason. After defeating the Portland Trailblazers 4-3 in the Western Conference Finals, the Lakers met the Indiana Pacers, led by veteran Reggie Miller, in the Finals. Thanks to Kobe's generalship and Shaq's MVP performance, Los Angeles got its first championship parade since the Magic Johnson era, and Kobe was finally starting to earn his comparisons to Michael Jordan.

Kobe takes on the Knicks at Madison Square Garden. In memory of one of the best to take the court there, the world's most famous arena turned its outer lights purple and gold when the world learned of his passing.

THE 2001 NBA CHAMPIONSHIP

BUILDING A DYNASTY

The 2000-2001 Philadelphia 76ers were a stacked team. Between offensive overlord Allen Iverson in his prime and defensive dominator Dikembe Mutombo in his twilight, the Eastern Conference champs looked like they might have been able to mount a valiant charge for the title against the defending champion Lakers. And though Iverson put up 48 points in a 76ers victory in Game 1, Kobe and the Lakers soon put an end to any talk of a challenge. Another MVP performance by Shaq coupled with Kobe's own team-high points totals in Games 2 and 3 gave the Lakers two in a row. A three-peat, however, was already beckoning for the Black Mamba.

THE 2002 NBA CHAMPIONSHIP
THREE-PEAT

Armed with the first overall draft pick in power forward Kenyon Martin and a hall-of-fame point guard in Jason Kidd, the New Jersey Nets were as prepared as any Eastern Conference team could have been for the Lakers as they made their way to the Finals. Kobe was, however, ready to shoot more than 50 percent from behind the arc, dish out assist after assist to Shaq and put up 26 ppg himself. The Lakers steamrolled the Nets, sweeping the series in four quick games despite Kidd's heroic efforts, including a triple-double in Game 1. Kobe had finally reached the Jordan-esque milestone of three championships in a row, and he had more than a decade left to play.

Kobe and Michael Jordan talk during a free-throw attempt during a December 17, 1997, game at the United Center in Chicago. Kobe scored a team-high 33 points while Jordan scored 36.

Kobe Bryant, Vanessa Bryant and their daughters Natalia and Gianna at Disneyland in 2010. In February of that year, Kobe passed Jerry West to become the Lakers' all-time leading scorer.

MOST VALUABLE PARENT

Off the court, Kobe poured his heart and essence into creating another lasting legacy: his family.

When the world first learned the tragic news that former Los Angeles Laker and basketball superstar Kobe Bryant, his 13-year-old daughter Gianna and several others lost their lives in a helicopter crash outside Calabasas, California, fans around the world rushed to pay their respects, mourning the sudden loss of one of basketball's greats. Some, however, were lucky enough to have known the man behind the jersey and the life he carved out as a devoted husband and proud father of four daughters.

In late 1999, when a 21-year-old Kobe opted to polish his musical prowess by recording the rap album *Visions*, his first and only foray into the music industry, the rising NBA star met and fell in love with Vanessa Laine, a backup dancer for Snoop Dogg's hip hop trio The Eastsidaz. After a whirlwind courtship, the couple married in 2001. Careful to maintain her family's privacy, Vanessa rarely granted interviews but was often seen accompanying Kobe to Lakers games, cheering on her increasingly successful husband as he dominated the court.

Vanessa soon gave birth to their first child: a daughter named Natalia. Over the years, the couple went on to welcome three more daughters to their growing family: Gianna, in 2006; Bianka in 2016; and Capri in 2019. A proud and doting father, Kobe often posted pictures and video clips of his girls to his social media accounts and, after joking about how he was "surrounded by women," he happily divulged he and his wife had been considering expanding their brood by trying for a boy. After announcing his retirement at the end of 2015, the celebrated shooting guard expressed his excitement at finally having more time to focus on his family.

Given her genetic pedigree, it perhaps came as no surprise that his second-eldest daughter, affectionately referred to as Gigi, began showing a budding aptitude for basketball at a young age. No stranger to sitting courtside, she aspired to follow in her father's footsteps. She dreamed of playing for the women's hoops powerhouse at the University of Connecticut in order to make a name for herself in the WNBA.

In a 2018 interview with Jimmy Kimmel, Kobe confided, "The best thing that happens is when we go out, and fans will come up to me, and she'll be standing next to me, and they will be like, 'You gotta have a boy, you and V [Vanessa] gotta have a boy, man, to have somebody carry on the tradition, the legacy.' And [Gigi] is like, 'I got this!' That's right...Yes, you do. You got this."

Kobe marked the beginning of his retirement by stepping onto the court not as a player, but as a coach. An encouraging mentor, he enjoyed taking Gigi to basketball practice, seeking to tutor and coach his daughter and support her firsthand. For the last two years, he helped train Gigi's Amateur Athletic Union team at the sports facility he helped cofound, the Mamba Sports Academy in Thousand Oaks, California. The two were en route to a tournament when their helicopter crashed, killing everyone aboard. A tragedy by any measure, it's made all the more devastating with the knowledge that they were all headed off to do something they loved.

THE 2008 MVP

KOBE STANDS ALONE

A fair number of critics thought that Kobe, at this point a 12-year NBA veteran, might lose the MVP award in 2008 to LeBron James, whose 30 ppg average was unmatched. Kobe, however, managed to come in just a few points shy of LeBron's total while also doing more to facilitate his teammates' scoring than he had ever done before. In the Lakers' triangle offense—the key to their three-peat earlier in the decade—assists were more evenly spread than points, allowing Kobe to tally 28 points, 6 rebounds and 5 assists per game in one of the finest all-around seasons in Laker history. Kobe's MVP award in 2008 was a once-in-a-lifetime recognition.

PIECES OF EIGHT

Over the course of his 20-year career, Kobe had a hand in designing dozens of shoes that bore his name, signed countless autographs and donned more Laker merch than Jack and Leo combined. Here are just a few selections, sold on Heritage Auctions over the years, that still carry some of his mystique.

2000 CHAMPIONSHIP RING
After their dynasty-starting championsip, the Los Angeles Lakers each received one of these diamond-studded rings.
Kobe would go on to add four more to his collection before retiring.

FULL AUTOGRAPH

This Spalding basketball signed by Kobe and auctioned off later is unique because, slammed for autographs as he was, Kobe was rarely able to sign his full name, usually opting for a shorter version to give as many fans as possible a chance to receive a souvenir.

A LEGEND IN TWO NUMBERS

Game-worn jerseys from Kobe's career are a prized memento among opposing players, who often trade jerseys after contests.

NIKE KOBE III

Given to Spike Lee when the filmmaker was collaborating with Kobe on his 2009 documentary *Kobe Doin' Work*, these priceless Kobe IIIs are a piece of Hollywood history as well as basketball lore.

COURT WORN

From his days with Adidas (above) to his latter day Nike revolution, Kobe's kicks were remarkable—even the ones he apparently hated.

FADE TO BLACK

For his final NBA game, Kobe received a one-of-a-kind pair of his signature sneaker, with an extremely limited number of replicas being released to lucky sneakerheads. The "Fade to Black" colorway pays homage to Kobe's Hollywood home and his superstar personality, with simple gold accents setting off the deep and final black of the upper and sole. Kobe wasn't even the only NBA player to don them on the court.

GAMEDAY DUNKS

Worn over the course of two games by Kobe during the 2008-2009 championship season, these kicks were later auctioned off.

Kobe talks with Head Coach Phil Jackson in a game against the Utah Jazz during the 2008 NBA Playoffs on May 9, 2008, at Energy Solutions Arena in Salt Lake City. Jackson was inducted into the Basketball Hall of Fame In 2007.

KOBE THE GOLDEN BOY

After a disastrous showing at the 2004 Athens games in which stars were eschewed in favor of younger talent, the 2008 U.S. Men's Olympic Basketball Team was ready to fire all of its big guns at once: Bryant, James, Kidd, Bosh, Paul and more were brought into the Olympic fold. They were the most talented group in the world, and they had grown up watching the storied 1992 Dream Team barrel through Barcelona on their way to Gold. They wanted their own. After a group stage that saw them defeat China, Angola, Greece, Spain and Germany in turn, the U.S. Men entered the tournament bracket. Australia and Argentina would fall to the stars and stripes before a final match against Spain and the Gasol brothers. Though Spain, led by Kobe's fellow Laker Pau Gasol, fought valiantly, Kobe and team USA beat them 118-107 to take the Gold.

VINCE BUCCI/AFP VIA GETTY IMAGES

Kobe and Shaq
on the court.
During their 2000
playoff run, the
pair combined
for more than 50
points per game.

THE END OF AN ERA: A REQUIEM FOR THE KOBE-SHAQ FEUD

On an episode of Shaquille O'Neal's "The Big Podcast," he and the Mamba finally put their past behind them.

The end of the Kobe-Shaq beef was monumental. Having witnessed it, we have all seen one of the great cease-fires in the history of civilization.

More heartfelt than the Christmas truce of 1914, more long-awaited than VE-Day or the Treaty of San Francisco, and more likely to prove factual than Dubya's famous proclamation of "Mission Accomplished," the end of an ongoing war between NBA basketball players Shaquille O'Neal and Kobe Bryant has been officially, diplomatically and permanently sealed on Shaq's podcast.

On an episode of "The Big Podcast with Shaq," hosted by the retired NBA center and current TNT television personality, Kobe and Shaq discussed their regrets about the feud. Shaq even introduced his former frenemy as "The Greatest Laker of All Time."

"A lot of stuff was said out of the heat of the moment," O'Neal said.

"Here's the thing, though," said Kobe. "When you say it at the time, you actually mean it, and then when you get older you have more perspective, and you're like holy s**t. I was an idiot when I was a kid."

Kobe and Shaq on the Laker bench. In 2012, Kobe played a charity game with Chinese celebrities in Shanghai, in which he scored 68 points in a 15-minute half.

The first (convincing) public show of reconciliation since their split, the podcast marks the end of the Shaq-Kobe feud, which has its own Wikipedia page.

Kobe and O'Neal were the greatest tandem in basketball since Michael Jordan and Scottie Pippen. As teammates for the Lakers, they won three consecutive championships from 2000-2002. In 2001, they rampaged through the NBA playoffs, losing only one game.

But there was trouble in paradise. Shaq, who joined the team in 1996 after leaving Orlando in free agency, felt that he was the franchise's cornerstone. In 2003, he started to demand a larger salary, all the while openly referring to himself using names

like "Superman," "The Big Diesel" and even "The Big Aristotle." He became famous in L.A. outside of basketball for his gregarious personality and interests in acting and music.

The ascendance of Kobe, who was drafted as a teenager after an illustrious high school basketball career, led to questions over who was truly the team leader. No slouch in the ego department himself, Kobe invented the phrase "taking my talent to [place]" and somehow convinced Brandy to accompany him to his high school prom.

Much like his idol Jordan, Kobe often clashed with teammates as a result of his relentless competitiveness.

With team chemistry already an issue from the

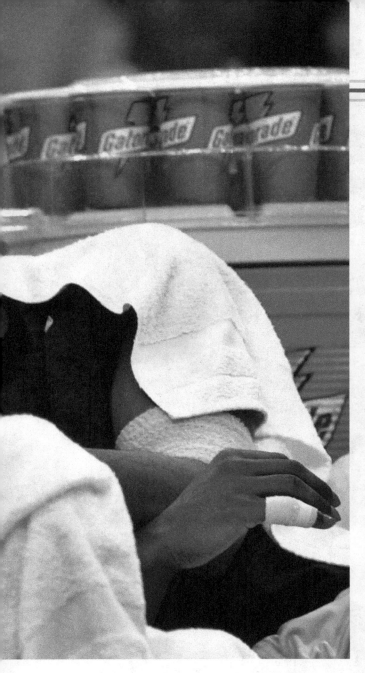

by brotherly love between two of the Lakers' most valued personalities.

From the *Newsweek* Archive 8/27/15
By Jack Martinez

MAKING UP

Excerpts from the podcast that ended the beef

SHAQ Listen, I think right now is time to clear the air. Because I've said many times that we were the most enigmatic, controversial, most talked about, dominant one-two punch. I just want people to know—I don't hate you, I know you don't hate me. I called it today a "work beef" is what we had. I was young, you was young. But then as I look at it—we won three out of four, so I don't really think a lot was done wrong. We had a lot of disagreements. We had a lot of arguments. But I think it fueled us. I was thinking at the end of the day, that's why Phil Jackson never really jumped in because he knew that you say something about me, I get pissed off. I say something off, you get pissed off. And again it works. I know we said a lot of crazy stuff, but I had fun doing it.

SHAQ Me and Kobe, we came in together. We were in Utah. Utah used to kill us all the time. Only one guy wanted to take the shot. I didn't want to take the shot. This guy took three major shots. He shot air balls. I knew then, you know what, this guy's not afraid.

KOBE You know what else? In '99, two things happened. I think Shaq realized, this kid is really competitive, and he's a little crazy. Then I realized that I probably had a couple of screws loose because we got in a fistfight and I actually was willing to get into a fistfight with this man. I went home and I was like, "Dude, I've got to be either the dumbest or the most courageous kid on the face of the earth."

SHAQ That just showed me that this kid ain't gonna back down. Kobe saw me punk everybody in the league! I knew then that, down by one, and I kick it out, he's gonna shoot it and he's gonna make it.

KOBE It was one of two things. Either he was going to beat the s**t out of me or I was going to get it done. I was comfortable either way.

beginning of the season, the Lakers imploded against the Detroit Pistons during the 2004 Finals in what is widely regarded as one of the most surprising outcomes in league history.

At that point, the Shaq-Kobe feud was already well-known. In practices, Kobe accused Shaq of caring more about money than the team and criticized his conditioning. Shaq, who'd requested a trade more than once, became so incensed by Kobe's attitude that he actually threatened to murder him, according to a Lakers PR representative.

Up until the podcast appearance, the two would still occasionally trade barbs in interviews. But the time since has been defined

Kobe on the bench at the Staples Center. The night of Kobe's passing, the Grammy Awards were held in the building. Host Alicia Keys delivered a memorial speech that can be found in part on page 86.

THE 2009 NBA CHAMPIONSHIP
NEW ERA, SAME MAMBA

The Orlando Magic and the Los Angeles Lakers earned their NBA Finals berths in 2009 through the Denver Nuggets and Cleveland Cavs respectively. The Magic seemed to be the team of destiny, having stopped LeBron's Eastern Conference juggernaut in its tracks. Kobe Bryant, however, still had his say. Averaging a whopping 32.4 points per game and 7.4 assists, Kobe proved his ability to take control of a basketball game was aging like wine. With more than 9 rebounds per game added to the Laker tally by Pau Gasol, the Magic never stood a chance. The series was over in five games, and Kobe had his first ring since the Shaq era.

ONE LAST DANCE

If Kobe had scripted his final NBA Championship win, he couldn't have done better than what happened in real life. Against his franchise's most storied rival, the Boston Celtics, Kobe averaged 28 points and 2 steals as the Lakers traded victories with the Celtics until a Game 7 was needed. Kobe would go on to add a second consecutive Finals MVP award for his heroics throughout the series, including a 10-point fourth quarter in Game 7 that cemented the Lakers' win. His fifth and final championship was also his most dramatic.

Kobe drives to the basket against the Denver Nuggets at the Staples Center on April 9, 2009, in Los Angeles. The Lakers won the game 116-102 with Kobe contributing 33 points.

Go to *OnNewsstandsNow.com*
for back issues of
![Newsweek] **Special Editions**

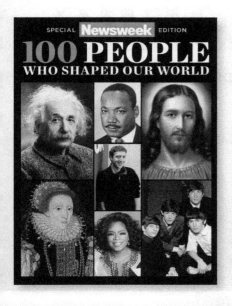

Collect all six!

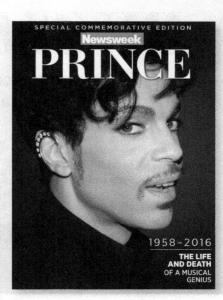

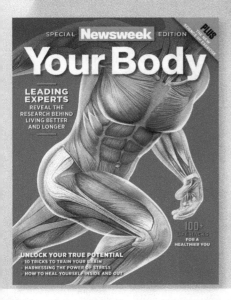

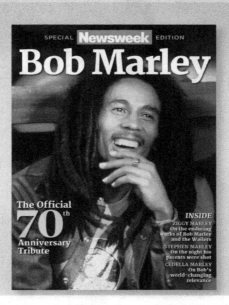

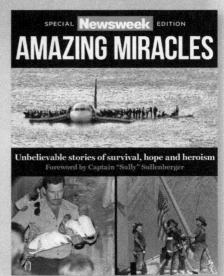

Plus the latest issues BEFORE they hit the newsstand!

NUMBER 24 BY THE NUMBERS

His stats on the court are just a few of the impressive digits associated with his legacy.

Number of languages in which Kobe Bryant was fluent. In addition to English, Kobe could speak both Italian (a direct result of being raised in the country) and Spanish.

29

Number of different NBA teams against which Kobe Bryant scored at least 40 points over the course of his career—every team in the league except the Lakers.

3

6

Number of times Kobe scored more than 60 points in a single game—including the last game in his career. Only Wilt Chamberlain (pictured) has more (32).

20 100

Number of seasons in Kobe's career, all of which he played as a Los Angeles Laker.

Percentage of NBA Slam Dunk contests in which Kobe Bryant has competed that he's also won. He remains the youngest player to have won the contest.

$328,238,062

Amount Kobe earned through his basketball contracts alone.

4

Kobe's place on the all-time list of NBA scorers. Kobe witnessed Laker LeBron James (pictured) take his place on the No. 3 spot, tweeting "Continuing to move the game forward @KingJames. Much respect my brother." He died the following day.

1

NBA players, outside of Kobe Bryant, who have spent 20 seasons with the same team. Dirk Nowitzki played for the Dallas Mavericks for 21 seasons.

2

Number of Kobe jerseys hanging in the rafters at the Staples Center, No. 8 and No. 24. He is the only NBA player to have received such an honor.

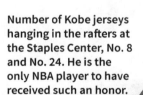

15-1

Kobe's record in the NBA Playoffs as part of a staggering run to claim the 2001 NBA Championship. The Lakers swept every team they faced as part of their march to the Finals, with only a 48 point performance from Allen Iverson in the first game of the Finals stopping the team from going undefeated. It remains the best postseason record of any NBA team.

THE 2012 OLYMPICS
A GOLDEN FINISH

After the U.S. Men's Olympic Basketball team's amazing show in 2008, London 2012 seemed like it might be a difficult forum for a repeat. That is, until you examined the U.S. roster: somehow even more impressive than its Beijing counterpart. Kobe was joined by Lebron, Kevin Love, Carmelo Anthony, Chris Paul, Kevin Durant, James Harden, Russell Westbrook, Deron Williams, Anthony Davis and Andre Iguodala. Harkening back to the 1992 Dream Team, the U.S. went undefeated in their Olympic campaign, beating Spain once again in the final. A fitting close to Kobe's international career, the London Games also stand out as one of Team USA's most dominating performances and secured a second gold medal for one of the game's most celebrated stars.

Kobe takes it to the basket against the Raptors' Matt Bonner on his way to an 81-point performance. Only Wilt Chamberlain's 100-point game stands above Kobe's that night.

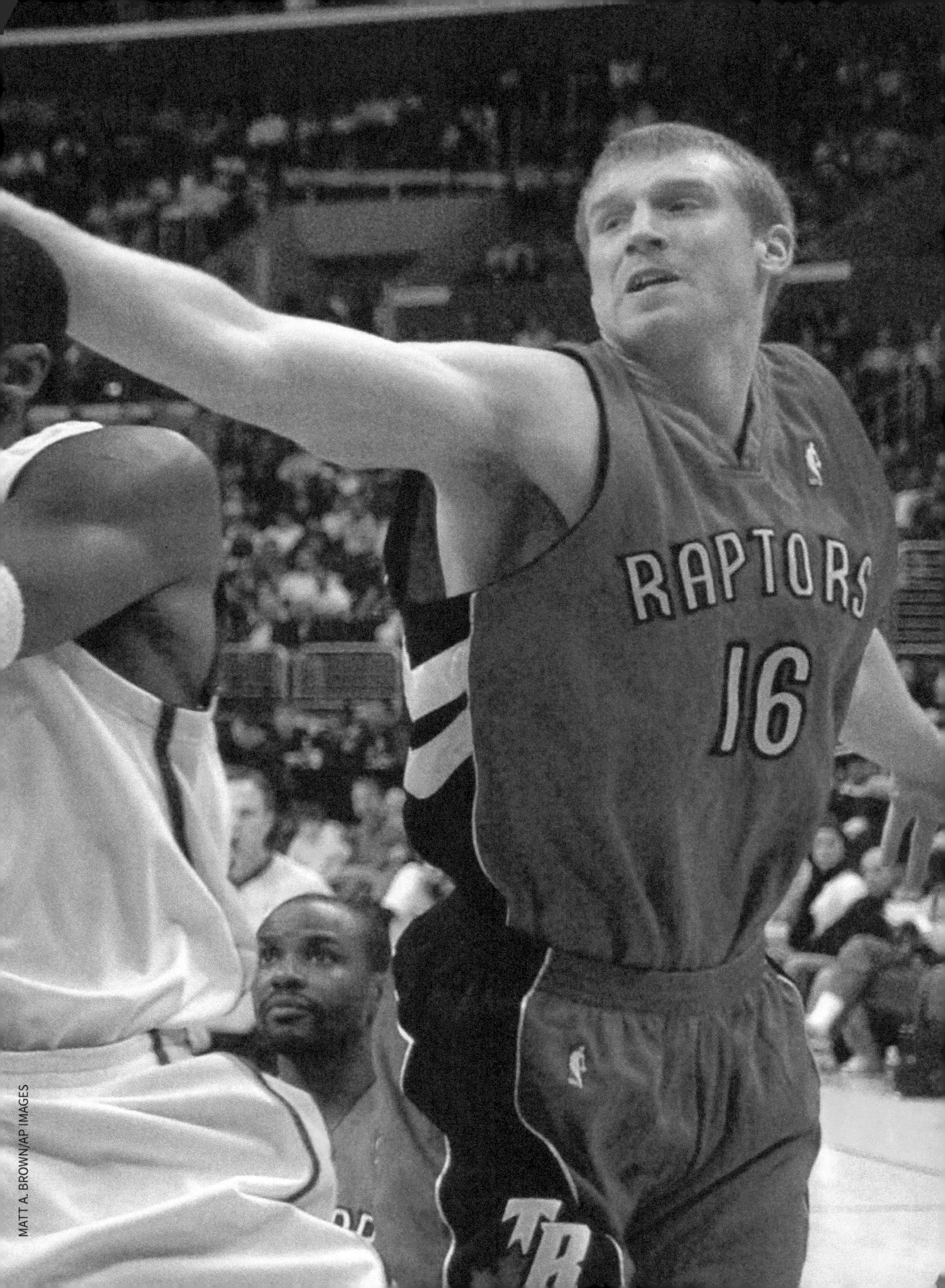

MATT A. BROWN/AP IMAGES

THE END OF THE LINE

When Kobe announced his retirement from basketball, he chose poetry as the medium to express the bittersweetness of the moment.

The *Players' Tribune* is a unique outlet in the world of sports journalism in that it publishes first-person narratives from athletes without the filter of a reporter. The resulting stories pull the curtain back on the world of pro athletics in a way that only those who take part in it every day can do. So it seemed perfect when Kobe chose *The Players' Tribune* to make the most important announcement of his career: about the nature of its end. Though he had hinted that the 2015-2016 season would be his last, Kobe had not made an official announcement until late November. When he did, it wasn't in the form of a press conference or a letter. It was a poem.

In clear language and lucid imagery, Kobe wrote 10 short verses entitled "Dear Basketball" in which he traced his love affair with the game from childhood until maturity. It was a piece of Kobe the inner man that fans got to see only on rare occasions when the fierce competitor was in repose—a condition that was anathema to his hard working spirit. Kobe wrote:

> **I played through the sweat and hurt**
> **Not because challenge called me**
> **But because YOU called me.**
> **I did everything for YOU**
> **Because that's what you do**
> **When someone makes you feel as**
> **Alive as you've made me feel.**

His verses show Kobe never viewed his career as something that happened to him: it was an entity unto itself. The game he loved was a living thing, and it constituted one of the most important relationships in his life. Over the course of the previous two seasons, Kobe had played in just 41 of 164 Laker games due to injury. Time was running short on his ability to compete at the highest level, but he was only grateful to the game. His verses are one of the most unorthodox retirement statements the world of sports has seen, but in retrospect it was perfect. Kobe summarized his time on the court and in the public eye better in verse than he ever could have in a speech. And now we get the immortal words to look back on:

> **You gave a six-year-old boy his**
> **Laker dream**
> **And I'll always love you for it.**
> **But I can't love you obsessively for**
> **much longer.**
> **This season is all I have left to give.**
> **My heart can take the pounding**
> **My mind can handle the grind**
> **But my body knows it's time to**
> **say goodbye.**
>
> **And that's OK.**
> **I'm ready to let you go.**
> **I want you to know now**
> **So we both can savor every moment**
> **we have left together.**
> **The good and the bad.**
> **We have given each other**
> **All that we have.**

Kobe Bryant reflects on his career during a press conference regarding his retirement on November 29, 2015. He earned a record four NBA All-Star game MVP awards, a distinction he shares with Bob Pettit.

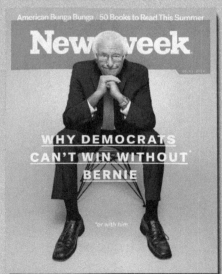

Newsweek.

HELPING YOU NAVIGATE A RAPIDLY CHANGING WORLD

| Award-winning journalists and photographers. | Download issues and read offline on any device. | National and global coverage on the issues that matter. | Expert analysis beyond the headlines on a wide range of topics. |

★ ★ ★ ★ ★

"I've been reading *Newsweek* since 1965. It is the source of much of my world knowledge. I find myself quoting it about once a week."

2 EASY WAYS TO SUBSCRIBE

▶ Go to **Newsweek.com/try** or complete and return this form.

→ Select One:

☐ **52 Weeks for $99**
($1.90 PER WEEK) 77% SAVINGS

☐ **104 Weeks for $179**
($1.72 PER WEEK) 79% SAVINGS

BEST OFFER!

RETURN TO:

NEWSWEEK SUBSCRIPTIONS DEPARTMENT
33 Whitehall Street, Floor 8
New York, NY, 10004

*Percentage savings calculated as a saving on our cover price, as found on the cover of Newsweek. The weekly price is an indication of what you will pay per issue, we will charge you the full price for the term you select.

Deliver to:

NAME

ADDRESS

CITY   REGION/STATE

ZIP CODE   COUNTRY

☐ Visa   ☐ Mastercard   ☐ Amex

CARD NO.

EXP.   CCV CODE

NAME ON CARD

SIGNATURE

To receive an email confirmation and other information, please provide your email address:

EMAIL

☐ **Payment enclosed** (checks made payable to Newsweek)

Kobe waves to the crowd as he is taken out of the game after scoring 60 points against the Utah Jazz at Staples Center on April 13, 2016.

A LAST VIRTUOSO PERFORMANCE

When he suited up for the Lakers for the last time in 2016, Kobe was already a living legend. Then he proved it anyway.

"I can't believe how fast 20 years went by," Kobe Bryant told the Staples Center crowd after his final NBA game on April 13, 2016. After expressing how much it meant to him that all 20 of those seasons had been spent on the team he loved as a boy, he added, "You can't write something better than this." Fans surrounded him, spilling out from the stands, as he said a final uniformed farewell to his office of two decades: the Staples Center hardwood. He was right: it was a picture-perfect ending to his career, and Los Angeles outdid themselves in showing their love for the departing hero. But Kobe also had a final show to put on, and he held up his part of the deal with interest.

After a career spent with critics snarling at him to pass more, Kobe chuckled during his farewell speech that on that night as the Lakers beat the Utah Jazz, Kobe's teammates were telling him over and over, "Don't pass it." Though the days when he could do so whenever he wanted seemed behind him, Kobe relished putting up 60 points one last time: an astronomical farewell from a man who delighted in such dominant performances more than any other aspect of the game. He'd once hit 50 in four consecutive games. He put up a scoreboard-scorching 81 against the Raptors over the course of a single game. But this last performance was something special. To score so many baskets in a game after seasons plagued by injury and atrophy parallels Beethoven writing his Ninth Symphony with hearing loss as much as it finds analog in the sporting world. In the fourth quarter, the Jazz had 21 total points. Kobe had 23. As his team trailed with time winding down, Kobe had 17 consecutive points. With 30 seconds left and the Lakers still down by one, he drained a three pointer that seemed inevitable to everyone in the arena, the Jazz included. One final bit of gamesmanship, one more victory by Kobe's hand and one more memory for 19,000 Laker fans packed into the Staples Center.

Kobe concluded his farewell speech with the simple words "Mamba Out" before blowing his fans, friends and family a kiss and dropping the mic at halfcourt. In the NBA, few players are afforded the luxury of deciding when they'll retire as opposed to teams deciding for them. Kobe is one of an even smaller number who was able to end his career as a living legend, showing at every point during his goodbye season exactly how much he meant to the game. His final, unforgettable performance was the perfect punctuation mark, complete with a mic drop that still echoes in the Staples Center.

Stills from the animated short film "Dear Basketball." In 2011, Kobe's career in film was foreshadowed when he became the first non-actor athlete to have his hand and footprints cemented at Grauman's Chinese Theatre in Hollywood.

DEAR BASKETBALL

A personal tribute to the game that changed his life, the animated short Kobe's poem inspired not only won an Oscar—it serves as a posthumous illustration of his passion for the sport.

When most players are ready to say farewell to the sports they love, they hold an emotional press conference. Kobe Bryant, enigmatic as ever, was not most players. Instead of gathering sports reporters and smiling through tears for the cameras to say goodbye, Kobe wrote a poem. "Dear Basketball," a personal essay posted on The Players' Tribune, declared the 2015-16 season would be the Black Mamba's last. Invoking the dreams of his childhood even as it acknowledges the toll time takes on us all, "Dear Basketball" celebrates the spirit of the sport as well as the intimacy that comes with true dedication—a feeling very few understand firsthand. And though the way in which the announcement took place was soon overshadowed by its consequences for fans of the player and the game, "Dear Basketball"'s journey was not yet complete.

Following his retirement, Kobe reached out to animator Glen Keane, a veteran of the industry who'd brought stories such as Disney's *Beauty and the Beast* to life with his sketches. Keane's stylized interpretation of Kobe's love letter, which depicts the star in his element at the height of his powers and also as a young boy deliberately dribbling and aching to dunk, is both a testament

to Kobe's lifelong passion for the game as well as a beautiful portrait of the many forms in which love can manifest itself. With a score by John Williams (whom Kobe asked to collaborate on the project because he wanted to impress his *Harry Potter*-soundtrack-obsessed daughters), the short is also an example of Kobe's relentless pursuit of excellence in anything he set his mind to. That hard work paid off. The short won the Academy Award for Best Animated Short, as well as the Annie Award—considered the highest achievement within the industry. The critical praise for "Dear Basketball" led many to assume Kobe was on the cusp of a promising second act as a media mogul and content creator. Like many things related to his death, the untapped potential for more work like "Dear Basketball" is a sad reminder of exactly what we lost.

Following Kobe's passing, Williams released a statement celebrating his friend and one-time collaborator: "During my friendship with Kobe, he was always seeking to define and understand inspiration even while modestly, and almost unknowably, he was an inspiration to countless millions.His enormous potential contribution to unity, understanding, and social justice must now be mourned with him."

Kobe makes a surprise visit to Oxford Preparatory Academy in Mission Viejo, California, in 2018. The school had recently made "The Punies," a podcast produced by Kobe's Granity Studios, part of its curriculum.

AN OSCAR FEELS BETTER THAN AN NBA CHAMPIONSHIP

After winning an Academy Award for "Dear Basketball," Kobe Bryant became the first person in history able to say the above with first-hand knowledge of both.

Retired NBA star Kobe Bryant was pretty adamant that the Oscar he won for an animated short was better than an NBA championship. Of course, when you've won five championship rings, maybe a new statue seems novel.

"I feel better than winning a championship, to be honest with you," Kobe told press after the big win for his short film titled "Dear Basketball." "I swear I do. Growing up, as a kid, I dreamt of winning championships and working really hard to make that dream come true.

"But then to have something like this seemingly come out of left field. I heard a lot of people tell me, when I started writing, they would ask me, 'What are you going to do when you retire?' And I'd say, 'Well I want to be a writer. I want to be a storyteller.' And I got a lot of, 'That's cute. That's cute,'" Kobe continued. "'You'll be depressed when your career's over, and you'll come back and play.' And I got that a lot. And to be here now and have this sense of validation, this is crazy, man. It's crazy."

Right after Kobe made his remarks, "Dear Basketball" animator Glen Keane cracked a joke about the physical toll of playing in the NBA.

"Not only that, after the win, you don't have to sit in the tub of ice," he said to Kobe, who spent more than one night in the tubs as a Laker.

Earlier in the evening, while accepting the Oscar for best animated short film, Kobe made headlines with a dig at Fox News host Laura Ingraham who said she thought NBA superstar LeBron James should "shut up and dribble" after he spoke out against President Donald Trump following having a racist slur painted on his home last year.

"I don't know if it's possible, I mean, as basketball players, we're really supposed to shut up and dribble," he said onstage. "I'm glad we do a little bit more than that."

From the *Newsweek* Archive 3/5/18
By Tim Marcin

FRAZER HARRISON/GETTY IMAGES

Kobe celebrates with his new hardware during the 2018 Academy Awards. His acceptance speech featured heartfelt thank yous in English and Italian.

From left: Magic Johnson, Jeanie Buss, Gianna Bryant, Vanessa Bryant, Kobe Bryant, Bianka Bryant, Natalia Bryant and Rob Pelinka during Kobe's retirement ceremony at the Staples Center in Los Angeles on December 18, 2017. Kobe is the only NBA player to have two numbers retired by the same team.

A SHOCKING GOODBYE

Kobe Bryant's death reverberated far beyond the world of sports and showed just how much impact he'd had during his 41-year life. Through tweets, Instagram stories, press releases and special moments outlined here, fans of Kobe expressed their admiration as well as a common sentiment: life is fleeting, and we should spend as much of it as we can with the people we hold most dear.

Bill Russell and Kobe Bryant share a laugh on the sidelines at the NBA All-Star Competition in Las Vegas, Nevada, February 17, 2007. In 2006, the Boston Celtics legend convinced Shaquille O'Neal to end his longtime feud with Bryant.

"Kobe was a leader of our game, a mentor to both male and female players. He gave his knowledge, time, and talent to tutor so many at the youth level, collegiate level, & NBA & WNBA players. Words can't express the impact that he had on the game of basketball. I know basketball fans all over the world will miss him, especially the City of Los Angeles....He was such an icon but also did so much for LA. He was passionate about serving the homeless and was an advocate for women's basketball. Coaching his daughter's basketball team brought him so much happiness."
—MAGIC JOHNSON

"Beyond devastated... my big brother... I can't, I just can't believe it."
—PAU GASOL

Atlanta Hawk Trae Young checked into the January 26 game against the Washington Wizards wearing No. 8 in honor of Kobe.

"He was great, charismatic & among the hardest-working athletes ever, but what impressed me most was how deeply-involved Kobe was with his 4 daughters. Pray for them, Vanessa, his parents & his fellow passengers' families on this sad and shocking day. We will never forget you Kobe."
—JIMMY KIMMEL

"WE HAVE TRAGICALLY LOST ONE OF THE GREATEST SPORTS FIGURES OF OUR TIME WITH THE PASSING OF KOBE BRYANT...THE GAME OF BASKETBALL IS BETTER TODAY BECAUSE OF KOBE, AND HE DESERVES ETERNAL APPRECIATION FOR THAT."
—MIKE KRZYZEWSKI

"Kobe was truly larger than life, a legend. May he and all those who lost their lives today rest in peace. Love and condolences to his family. LA will never be the same."
—LEONARDO DICAPRIO

"JEANNINE & I ARE ABSOLUTELY SHOCKED TO HEAR OF THE LOSS OF ONE OF MY FAVORITE PEOPLE & ONE OF THE BEST BASKETBALL MINDS IN THE HISTORY OF THE GAME! OUR HEARTS & PRAYERS TO VANESSA & HIS GIRLS.@KOBEBRYANT YOU WERE MY BIGGEST FAN, BUT I WAS YOURS"

—BILL RUSSELL

"I'm so sad and stunned right now. In Staples Arena, where Kobe created so many memories for all of us, preparing to pay tribute to another brilliant man we lost too soon, Nipsey Hussle. Life can be so brutal and senseless sometimes. Hold on to your loved ones. We miss you, Kobe"
—JOHN LEGEND

"IT'S VERY DIFFICULT FOR ME TO PUT IN WORDS HOW I FEEL... KOBE WAS AN INCREDIBLE FAMILY MAN, HE LOVED HIS WIFE AND DAUGHTERS, HE WAS AN INCREDIBLE ATHLETE... HE INSPIRED A WHOLE GENERATION. THIS LOSS IS, IT'S JUST HARD TO COMPREHEND."
—KAREEM ABDUL-JABBAR

"Earlier today, Los Angeles, America and the whole wide world lost a hero. We're literally standing here heartbroken in the house that Kobe Bryant built...We're gonna love together and we're gonna make sure we celebrate the most powerful energy—the one thing that has the power to bring us all together: And that's music. It's the most healing thing in the world."
—ALICIA KEYS *during the Grammy Awards on Sunday, January 26 at the Staples Center. Keys and Boyz II Men sang "It's So Hard to Say Goodbye to Yesterday" as a tribute to Kobe during the awards show.*

"You know he means a lot to me, obviously. He was such a great opponent. It's what you want in sports. He had that DNA that very few athletes can ever have — the Tiger Woods, the Michael Jordans. I was getting to know him since he retired. This is a tough one."
—DOC RIVERS

Dwyane Wade and Kobe Bryant share a courtside moment at the Staples Center in Los Angeles, California, February 28, 2008. The two star players won gold as part of the USA Basketball team at the Beijing Olympics later that year.

"We are shocked and saddened by the devastating news of the passing of Kobe Bryant and his daughter, Gianna. Kobe was an ambassador for our game, a decorated legend and a global icon. Above all, he was a loving and dedicated father. Kobe's legacy transcends basketball, and our organization has decided that the number 24 will never again be worn by a Dallas Maverick. Our hearts go out to all the lives lost and the families impacted by this terrible tragedy. We send our thoughts and prayers to Vanessa and the family, the Lakers organization and Kobe Bryant fans everywhere."
—MARK CUBAN

The Italian basketball federation declared a minute of silence would be observed before every game for a week following Kobe's death.

"I CAME IN THE LEAGUE AND I CHASED HIM. THAT'S WHO I CHASED. I WANTED TO BE RESPECTED BY HIM, AND ONCE I REACHED THAT LEVEL, I KNEW I DID SOMETHING. KOBE, THANK YOU, MAN. THANK YOU FOR ALL THE MEMORIES — WE'VE GOT A LOT OF GOOD ONES. THESE TEARS THAT WE CRY, WE'RE GOING TO MISS YOU. AND IT'S NOT LEAVING TODAY, A WEEK FROM NOW, A MONTH FROM NOW, A YEAR FROM NOW. WE'LL FOREVER, FOREVER MISS YOU, MAN. YOU'RE A LEGEND, YOU'RE AN ICON, YOU'RE A FATHER, YOU'RE A HUSBAND, YOU'RE A SON, YOU'RE A BROTHER, YOU'RE A FRIEND. THANK YOU FOR BEING MY FRIEND. I LOVE YOU, BROTHER."
—DWYANE WADE

"I'm heartbroken by this news, you were a true legend, and friend. Rest In Peace, @kobebryant."
—TONY PARKER

"There are no words to express the pain I'm going through now with this tragic and sad moment of losing my niece Gigi & my brother, my partner in winning championships, my dude and my homie. I love you and you will be missed. My condolences go out to the Bryant family and the families of the other passengers on board. I'm sick right now."
—SHAQUILLE O'NEAL

"Where we think everything's solid, there's a big hole in the wall. I was used to seeing and talking to Kobe that — it kills you. It's just a terrible event."
—JACK NICHOLSON

Several NBA teams playing games on Sunday, January 26, took intentional 24-second violations in order to honor Kobe.

"He taught me so many things in life that were necessary on and off the court. On the court, he taught me how to carve out defenses and how to take my time. How to make winning my ultimate goal. Off the court, he taught me to sign my own checks lol. I'm glad I got to be the yin to your yang as far as the locker room was concerned."
—LAMAR ODOM

Kobe Bryant presents President Barack Obama with a Lakers jersey at the White House on January 25, 2010. The same year, Obama teamed up with Kobe to fill care packages at an NBA Cares service event at the Boys and Girls Club in Washington, DC.

"KOBE WAS A LEGEND ON THE COURT AND JUST GETTING STARTED IN WHAT WOULD HAVE BEEN JUST AS MEANINGFUL A SECOND ACT. TO LOSE GIANNA IS EVEN MORE HEARTBREAKING TO US AS PARENTS. MICHELLE AND I SEND LOVE AND PRAYERS TO VANESSA AND THE ENTIRE BRYANT FAMILY ON AN UNTHINKABLE DAY."

—BARACK OBAMA

"I LOVED KOBE—HE WAS LIKE A LITTLE BROTHER TO ME. WE USED TO TALK OFTEN, AND I WILL MISS THOSE CONVERSATIONS VERY MUCH. HE WAS A FIERCE COMPETITOR, ONE OF THE GREATS OF THE GAME AND A CREATIVE FORCE. KOBE WAS ALSO AN AMAZING DAD WHO LOVED HIS FAMILY DEEPLY — AND TOOK GREAT PRIDE IN HIS DAUGHTER'S LOVE FOR THE GAME OF BASKETBALL."
—MICHAEL JORDAN

"I didn't understand why people in the gallery were saying, 'Do it for Mamba.' Now I understand. It's a shocker to everyone. I'm unbelievably sad, and it's one of the more tragic days. The reality is setting in because I was just told about 5 minutes ago.

Life is very fragile as we all know. You can be gone at any given time and we have to appreciate the moments that we have."
—TIGER WOODS

"The crash was a tragedy for multiple families. My heart goes out to Vanessa and the families that lost loved ones. Kobe was a chosen one—special in many ways to many people. Our relationship as coach/player transcended the norm. He went beyond the veil."
—PHIL JACKSON

The futbol club AC Milan will wear black armbands in its upcoming cup game to honor Kobe, a lifelong fan of the team.

"All of us know what a great player he was, but he went beyond great playing. He was a competitor—that goes unmatched. And it's what made him as a player so attractive to everybody—that focus, that competitiveness, that will to win. And even more importantly than that, we all feel a deep sense of loss for what he meant to all of us in so many ways, and so many millions of people loved him for so many different reasons. It's just a tragic thing."
—GREG POPOVICH

On Saturday, January 25, 2020, the day before Kobe's death, LeBron James became the NBA's third-highest scoring player of all time. Speaking after the game, he said:

"I'm happy just to be in any conversation with Kobe Bean Bryant. One of the all-time greatest basketball players to ever play, one of the all-time greatest Lakers."

"I haven't come to grips with this. First you have a feeling of shock, then a feeling of horrible sorrow, and then you start having all these recollections of the times I shared with him. Unbelievable. Just unbelievable. I feel like I've lost a son."
—JERRY WEST

"I HAVE NO WORDS...ALL I HAVE IS REAL TEARS....THIS IS BEYOND HEARTBREAKING."
—KEVIN HART

"Man this is a tough one for me! You were the first guy to put me under your wing and show me the ins and outs of the league. Had so many great convos about so many things and I will cherish those moments forever. Love you forever, Bean!"
—ANTHONY DAVIS

"For 20 seasons, Kobe showed us what is possible when remarkable talent blends with an absolute devotion to winning. He was one of the most extraordinary players in the history of our game with accomplishments that are legendary: Five NBA championships, an NBA MVP award, 18 NBA All-Star selections, and two Olympic gold medals. But he will be remembered most for inspiring people around the world to pick up a basketball and compete to the very best of their ability. He was generous with the wisdom he acquired and saw it as his mission to share it with future generations of players, taking special delight in passing down his love of the game to Gianna. We send our heartfelt condolences to his wife, Vanessa, and their family, the Lakers organization and the entire sports world."
—ADAM SILVER

UPI/ROGER L. WOLLENBERG/ALAMY

On November 17, 2019, Kobe and Gianna Bryant were courtside at the Staples Center to watch LeBron and the Lakers take on the Atlanta Hawks. LeBron passed Kobe's all-time points total on January 25.

Kobe celebrates during
the season opening
game against the Los
Angeles Clippers at
Staples Center on
October 27, 2009.
The Lakers beat their
hometown rivals 99-92.

FIRST BALLOT

This year, the basketball world will gather to enshrine Kobe in the Basketball Hall of Fame.

Outside the Naismith Basketball Hall of Fame in Springfield, Massachusetts, on January 26, the marquee bore a simple message: KOBE. Throughout his career, Kobe had cemented the case that he belonged in the hallowed halls of Springfield. His induction later this year, inevitable according to the basketball world, was one of the most anticipated in recent memory both because Kobe was among the best speechmakers in NBA history and because his fellow first-ballot inductees were likely to include Kevin Garnett and Tim Duncan. Now, the ceremony will be colored by a much different mood than Laker fans had anticipated, but the honor will be no less deserved or important despite being posthumous. His time with the Lakers, illustrated by the statistics at right, constituted a career that ranks among the longest and most decorated in league history. His enshrinement in the Hall of Fame will no doubt be a somber occasion, but it will give his legacy yet another place—in addition to the courts and arenas all over the country where he made his mark—to live on.

KEVORK DJANSEZIAN/GETTY IMAGES

A CAREER IN THE SPOTLIGHT

Games Played 1,346 (14th all time)
Minutes Played 48,637 (7th all time)
Career Points 33,643 (4th all time)
Career Field Goals 11,719 (5th all time)
Career 3-Pointers 1,827 (11th all time)
Free Throws Made 8,378 (3rd all time)
50-Point Games 26 (3rd all time)
Steals 1,944 (16th of all time)
15-time All-NBA Team Selections
18-time NBA All-Star
34-time Player of the Month
4-time All-Star Game MVP (Tied for Record)
*Only Player in NBA History to score 600 points
    in three consecutive postseasons*
2nd Youngest Player to Score 33,000 Points
Oldest Player to Score 60 Points in a Game
Most Points Scored in Lakers Franchise History

A Topix Media Lab Publication
For inquiries, call 646-476-8860

CEO Tony Romando

Senior Vice President of Sales & New Markets Tom Mifsud
Vice President of Retail Sales & Logistics Linda Greenblatt
Director of Finance Vandana Patel
Manufacturing Director Nancy Puskuldjian
Financial Analyst Matthew Quinn
Brand Marketing & Promotions Assistant Emily McBride

Editor-in-Chief Jeff Ashworth
Creative Director Steven Charny
Photo Director Dave Weiss
Managing Editor Courtney Kerrigan

Issue Editor Tim Baker
Art Director Susan Dazzo
Associate Editors Trevor Courneen, Juliana Sharaf
Designer Kelsey Payne
Copy Editor & Fact Checker Tara Sherman
Associate Photo Editor Catherine Armanasco

Co-Founders Bob Lee, Tony Romando

Global Editor in Chief Nancy Cooper
Creative Director Michael Goesele
Executive Editor Mary Kaye Schilling
Deputy Editors Laura Davis, Michael Mishak
Special Projects Editor Fred Guterl

CEO Dev Pragad

Newsweek LLC

ISBN: 978-1-948174-63-3

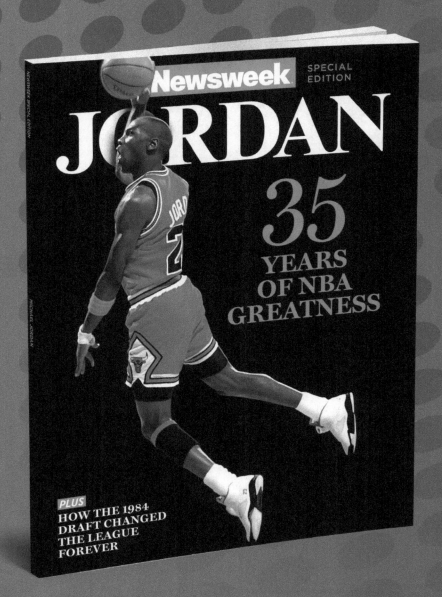

From left: Elden Campbell, Shaquille O'Neal, Eddie Jones and Kobe Bryant. Jones switched from No. 25 to No. 6 after his second season with the Lakers after the team retired 25 for Gail Goodrich.

Kobe at the Euro ABC camp in Berlin, Germany, on July 7, 1999. Kobe chose the number 8 as it represented the sum of the numbers he wore at the camp as a youth: 1, 3 and 4.

CPSIA information can be obtained
at www.ICGtesting.com
Printed in the USA
BVHW011413210520
580082BV00009B/641